MY FIGHT WITH THE DEVIL

DERRICK TURNER

ISBN
978-1-957378-69-5 (Paperback)
978-1-957378-68-8 (eBook)
978-1-957378-70-1 (Hardcover)

TABLE OF CONTENTS

CHAPTER 1

"NORMAL," what the hell does that mean! Don't waste your time trying to figure it out. I'm 54 years old and I still don't have a fucking clue! They say, "we learn from our parents," well let me expound on that…

The first thing my parents taught me was how to mask all the dysfunctional shit they were doing. Getting drunk, cussing each other out, fighting, and everything else you can think of. I mean, my life was anything but normal. But when you're nine, ten, eleven years old, seeing your parents drunk was funny. My father would come home wasted and crack jokes until the liquor stretched him out in the middle of the bathroom floor, his arms wrapped tightly around the porcelain god. I remember him asking the toilet to save him from the sickness he was feeling. I remember standing there, waiting to see if the toilet would free him from his anguish. It would be years before I learned the devil came in many forms, and his force would soon come cleverly disguised in a cloud of white smoke!

I was around seven years old when I saw the evil slither its way into my home. Of course I didn't know it at the time, but it was the devil riding my parents back like a cowboy at a rodeo. As a kid I was taught the devil was this creature who stood upright like a man and his skin was fiery red, and he had huge fangs, horns on his head,and a long pointed tail that protruded from his lower back, and he held a large red hot fork in his hand that he used to carry the condemned to his dungeon consumed by fire to be punished for all eternity for their sins.

At seven years old my curiosity was off the charts. As scary as the description of him sounded, I remember wanting to see this hideous beast in the flesh. I had no idea he was already there, lurking in the souls of my own parents. They had been prisoners to this unholy entity for years, probably even before I was born. My father lied, my mother lied, and they dressed up the truth to blind me from the reality of the hell we were all trapped in.

I never knew hell could be above ground, but in my household it was just that. The only thing missing was the fire. The physical abuse was overwhelming when it came to life right in front of my eyes! My father was the man of the house and the way he enforced his dominance was with violence and my mother was his punching bag. I hated when I saw him hit my mother, but the fights would only seem to happen when he had been drinking. Sober, he was my best friend, but the liquor turned him into a force to be reckoned with. At seven years old, he was a huge man and I feared him! I didn't understand addiction and I didn't know he was an alcoholic.

I remember those days I would run to the living room window, gazing out at his parking space, waiting on him to come home from work. Those were some of the best times of my life because I knew he hadn't been drinking yet and my mother would not have to suffer any abuse. He had his flaws and some of them were ugly, but he was my father. He was the example I had to follow, and he demonstrated it with an iron fist!

I believe the mental abuse started before I was seven, but I was too young to know what it was. I mean, they talked to one another using such harsh words, but soon after, they would be laughing and in love as though nothing ever happened. That was the part that always confused me. I didn't understand how you could beat someone and love them at the same time.

My mother always made excuses for my father's abuse. "It's the alcohol," she would say. I was too young to know how to separate the two. She would take those beatings from my father like a child being spanked by his parents and knew not to swing back! The flights were devastating on the weekends because saturday and sunday were his off days. He started drinking around two or three in the afternoon. The liquor fueled his anger and sent him into a furious rage! I was seven years old and no match for the beast that emerged out of him. I had to watch him strike my mother with a closed fist and there wasn't a damn thing I could do to stop him. The physical abuse hadn't landed in my lap yet, but sometimes I wish it had, the mental abuse was much worse.

As I grew older the fights came more frequent and more violent. His drinking progressed, and his punches started rerouting in my direction. I was around ten or eleven the first time he hit me.......

He came home late one Friday evening wasted! I was posted in front of the living room window the way I did every night since I was 5 years old. I always knew when he was parking; his car had a unique sound and it was programmed in my hearing. He opened the car door and got out stumbling and tripping over his own feet. I knew as soon as he entered the house my mother was his target. But, I was wrong, he opened the front door and the moment I saw his face I knew he was dead drunk. All though I had grown a little, I was still no match for the rage in him. The thought of fighting him back was just that, a thought; I knew if I raised a hand against him he would hurt me bad, or maybe even kill me! The swift punches flashed in my memory. All the times I had seen him hit my mother, came rushing back to reality when I looked at him. His face had an ugly snarl, and his fists were clenched and ready to strike! I don't know where I got the courage from, but I wasn't about to stand by and watch him beat my mother again.

I took a seat on the living room couch and waited patiently for the violence to erupt. I knew there was no way I could beat him, but there was one way I could stop this nightmare from continuing, I could kill'em! I had thought about killing him before, but, somehow he would win back my love for him and the thought would go away. It was always a trick, the good times never lasted long and his rage seemed to always be at its peak. But, this day was different, I was fed up with the abuse and I refused to allow it anymore. I watched him closely as he staggered his way to the kitchen where my mother was. The strong smell of liquor followed him like a dim cloud. The closer he got to the kitchen, the more intense I became. The anticipation of what I knew was about to happen, overwhelmed me. It was now or never, I had to get up and get to him before he reached my mother or it would be too late. I stood up, flexing my immature muscles, trying to prepare them for battle, when suddenly he turned and faced me. His face was occupied by a look that I had never seen before. He seemed to be possessed by something or someone unholy. His eyes were bloodshot red and his skin looked wrinkled and scorched. For some reason he seemed taller and more scarier than I'd ever seen him. The muscles in face pulsated like a heartbeat, but much more violently. He stared at me, his devilish eyes pierced my soul! There was no time to rationalize my next move, I had to stop him or watch him beat my mother again; and then it hit me like a ton of bricks, he was preparing to attack me.

He batted his eyes like he was trying to focus. The liquor had his sight crossed up and his balance was off severely. This was the drunkest I'd ever seen him. He started to walk toward me, but he couldn't keep his feet in line; and then I noticed. He wasn't trying to get to me, he was trying to get to his bedroom where his gun was. I had experienced that before; he had held my mother at gunpoint a few times, but somehow he always turned it into a joke. This time was different, he had every intention of hurting me and I knew it. I had to get to the bedroom before him, but my courage failed me and I froze like a block of ice, I couldn't move and my fear granted him the opportunity to carry out his mission.

I heard him rambling in the room looking for the weapon. It was a small 38 caliber snub nose pistol he had bought for my mom to carry with her to and from work. The rambling stopped, and he exited the room with the gun in his hand, aiming it right at me. I couldn't run, hell, I couldn't move! My feet were glued to the floor in fear. I tried to open my mouth to warn my mother, but I knew if I uttered a word he would pull the trigger.

He stumbled forward, keeping his aim he pointed the gun directly at my chest. The closer he got the more my adrenaline escalated until he was close enough for me to fight for my life. I closed my eyes and swung at the hand holding the gun. The look of shock dilated his pupils as the gun flew across the room hitting the wall. I hadn't anticipated my reactions, it just happened. Suddenly, I found myself standing face to face with something other than my father. His face twisted, his eyes bloodshot red and his stare cold and penetrating.

We both looked at the gun at the same time, but neither of us advanced toward it. We just stood there, froze in the moment.

Fear captivated me, but I couldn't figure out what stopped him. His rage was at its peak, but he wasn't reacting to it. He seemed furiously angry, but too wasted to attack. It was the first time I'd seen him hesitate, he had never done this before.

I took advantage of the delay in his rage. But, it was a set up; as soon as I suspended the animation in my stiff body, he rushed me with extreme force, knocking me against the living room sofa and the attack began!

The punches were coming slow and off target. The liquor had him sloppy and discombobulated. But, he was determined to show no mercy. I hit the wall head first, causing my vision to double. Although I feared him, now wasn't the time to be scared; weak or not, I had to fight back.

He sensed the fear and rushed me a second time, but this time I was prepared. I side stepped him as he tripped over his own feet. Trying to regain his balance, he tripped a second time, this time his head grazed the corner of the cocktail table, cutting him above his right eye. The meeting with the table had no effect on him, he kept coming. Blood poured from the wound as he wiped it away trying to focus on my position.

The gun was only a foot away from me and I had only one opportunity to get it while he shook off the effects of the fall. The down side of his drinking binge was starting to weaken him and the nausea that came with it began to take its place in the pit of his stomach. It wouldn't be long before the porcelain god beckoned him to his knees and he would be totally helpless.

I sat down on the living room sofa with the gun in my hand while I listened to him throwing up his insides in the bathroom toilet. This was the perfect time for me to inflict back some of the pain he'd put my mother through. He was at his weakest point and I knew it was my time to strike back. Fear wasn't an option, I had to do it!

I stood up, gripping the gun tightly in my hand. I was only eleven years old, but the violence I'd experienced in my own home prepared me for what I needed to do, kill him! This could be the day it all ended, it was my chance to free my mother from the hell she was trapped in.

Suddenly the vomiting stopped, but the stench reeked from the bathroom like a decomposed body. I snatched the bathroom door open and aimed the gun directly at his head. He was so wasted, he didn't even see me standing there. The fear escaped me, and visions of his beatings swam through my mind like a violent storm. I pulled the trigger, but nothing happened. I pulled it again, nothing. He lifted his head and stared at me with vengeance in his eyes. I was holding an unloaded gun.

He stood up, wiping the vomit from his lips, he lunged at me with all he had. This time the blows came swiftly, each one hitting its target. I tried to cover up, but the attack was too vicious and my small frame was no match for the beast he'd become. I remember one of the punches landing beneath my rib cage, taking the wind from my body! I hit the floor and bald up in a fetal position, gasping for air. The tears started filling up in the web of my eyes, but, I refused to let him see me cry, it would only make the beating worse.

Finally, the unjust punishment stopped, but the pain in my ribs was excruciating! Every time I inhaled, it felt like I was being stabbed repeatedly. He took one last glance at me, and walked out, slamming the door behind him. I had to get up, he was gonna attack my mother next. I grabbed the side of the tub for support, my ribs were broken no doubt. I pushed against the tub slowly until I could stand without something assisting me.

I opened the door slowly, anticipating him on the other side waiting to continue his reign of terror. I looked behind me at the gun on the floor, but it wouldn't be of any use to me, it wasn't loaded. I was in too much pain to challenge him, so I stood there, peaking through the crack in the door like a frightened little kid.

I tensed up, anticipating the physical abuse to continue with my mother. Ten or fifteen minutes must have passed by, and I heard nothing. It hadn't dawned on me why my mother hadn't come to my rescue the entire time he was attacking me, especially since she had promised never to let him lay a hand on me. Where was she; had she left me alone? Did she go out the back door for help? Was she hiding somewhere in the house, listening to me fight for my life? This was her fight, she was responsible for his rage, not me!

Finally, I emerged from the bathroom and cautiously approached the kitchen, but I didn't see her, she wasn't there. It wasn't the first time he had gone into a rage, but I never knew her to run, even when she knew she couldn't beat him she stood firm.

His focus was on finding her, he didn' even hear me come out of the bathroom. I watched him exit the back door, and I seized the opportunity to lock him out. I had to find the bullets for the gun. Even if I wasn't going to kill'em I didn't want him to get his hands on them.

Usually the liquor would have taken effect and he would be in the bed sleeping it off. But, he was on a rampage and all I wanted to do was find my mother and get the hell outta there. I moved through the house swiftly calling her name, but there was no response.

The house was strangely silent, and I couldn't see my father through the back door window anymore. I didn't know where my mother was, but I had to focus on finding those bullets. I knew when he came back I was gonna need that gun, it was the only thing I had to protect me from him. Even if I didn't have the courage to use it, I felt safe knowing I had it and he didn't.

There was only one place they could be, and that was in my mother's room, so I started my search there. I knew he kept the shells for his shotgun in the bedroom closet on the shelf. As soon as I turned on the bedroom light I saw them. I loaded the gun and took a seat at the kitchen table, waiting for him to return. Hopefully the downside of his drunken stupor had gotten the best of him and he would be too worn out to fight.

While I waited for him, I took the opportunity to pour out all the liquor he had sitting around the house. I knew all his stash spots, I would watch him hide it, my mother was too scared to touch it. I didn't really wanna hurt him, he was my dad. I just wanted him to sober up and stop the abuse.

CHAPTER 2

It was four or five o'clock in the morning when my mother finally came walking through the front door. I was still sitting at the kitchen table holding the gun in my hand, staring out the back door window ready to shoot if I had to.

It was Saturday Morning and usually these drinking binges lasted the whole weekend. But, now he had started to attack me. No one ever knew what went on behind closed doors, if my mother or I said anything the abuse would get worse. What happened inside, stayed inside. We were living with the devil in human form.

I didn't tell my mother about the fight my father and I had, it would only add to the stress she was already dealing with. Although I was upset with her for leaving me there to face him alone, I didn't hold it against her, he would have beaten her to. The fights had gotten the best of her, it was starting to show on her face. She was losing weight, and she cried all the time. I could only imagine how long she had been suffering from his foul behavior. I remember my brother and sister telling me they went through the same thing, and they were much older than me. But, they were grown now, with families of their own, they didn't have to endure it anymore.

Thank God his drinking binges only happened on the weekends, I don't know what my mother and I would have done if we had to live with it everyday. How she found the strength to endure his attacks, I will never know. For thirty plus years she stood in the ring with him toe to toe, absorbing the blows from his huge hands, sometimes knocking her off her feet. He was the prince of evil, and the liquor was his sidekick.

I sat at the kitchen table in pain from the blow to my ribs. It was the first time he'd ever hit me and I knew it wasn't gonna stop. I had to convince my mother to leave him or I was sure he was gonna kill us both. But, she was in love with evil, an emotion I knew nothing about, nor did I understand it. In my house love demonstrated itself with black eyes and busted lips.

My mother talked about God all the time and how he was this spirit who watched over us and was supposed to keep us safe from harm and danger, but we couldn't see him. All we had to do was ask for his help and somehow things would change. I remember watching her kneel down on her bedroom floor and pour her heart out to God and nothing happened. If he was real, why wasn't he helping us? Was she being punished for something she'd done I knew nothing about? If so, what did it have to do with me? Why was I being punished?

I had my moments when I tried talking to God, asking him to save us from my dad. Sometimes I even asked him to help my father stop drinking. But, it never worked. He had been a drunk all my life, and I honestly didn't think anything or anyone could make him change. I had no faith in his recovery.

I sat there, captivated by everything I'd just gone through. My mother walked in the kitchen and sat down next to me. I could tell from the look in her eyes she was sorry for leaving me there with him. She had no Idea I had taken a beating, she just sat there staring at me, speechless.

It didn't take long for her to figure it out, I couldn't mask the pain I was in and it showed on my face. She was responsible for the torture I'd endured and she did nothing to stop it. I had been born into a world of shit and there was not a damn thing I could do about it! I was young and confused and none of it made sense. We were victims of an evil we didn't understand, and I was sure we never would. It was like a movie and my mother and I played the worst parts.

We both sat there suspended in time. I could tell by the look in her eyes she was anticipating his return to be much more violent than the last. I had never seen her that scared before, she was terrified, her hands were shaking and her eyes were roaming all over the house in fear!

Finally, she got up and tried to prepare herself for work. She was exhausted and restless. I had no idea where she had been, but she had this puzzling look on her face; she looked as though she didn't know where she was. She looked at me like I was a total stranger, like I wasn't supposed to be there.

I stood up with the gun in my hand, letting her know if he came back, I was prepared to defend us. The violence had to stop, but it wouldn't matter if she refused to leave. What was it gonna take to convince her if we stayed he would surely kill us!

She came outta her room fully dressed for work. Her pupils were dilated the size of dime as she gazed at her surroundings. She walked into the kitchen and opened the refrigerator and grabbed a beer. It was her only escape mentally from the situation she was in. She sat at the kitchen table and drank them one after the other. It always amazed me how she could drink so many and never seemed drunk. She took her last swallow and left for work. Again I was alone, just me and the revolver.

I got up to check the front door to make sure it was locked, I wanted to make sure I heard him when he came in. I looked at the beer cans she left on the table and shook them one by one, making sure they were all empty. The last one I picked up was half full. It was my opportunity to see what the secret was, what was in it that calmed my mother so. Before I knew it, the can met my lips and the cold and bitter wetness lit up my taste buds like a flash of lighting, I was hooked from the very first drink.

I finished it and grabbed another one, and another one, and another one. I didn't know it at the time, but that's the day I LET THE DEVIL IN.

The taste was new to me and I liked it. I wasn't sure what to expect, I guess I was looking for a feeling other than the usual. I was confused. The liquor seemed to calm my mother, but enraged my father. I opened the fridge to look for more, and there they were, lined up like soldiers ready for battle, and for that brief moment I was the sergeant in charge.

The beer started to take effect shortly after I drank it. I noticed my vision starting to double and my balance was off. It Reminded me of how my father would be when he was drunk, staggering all over the house. It was my first time,so I didn't know my limit, I just kept drinking until I washed away all the unwanted emotions and bad memories of abuse dend neglect that plagued my life. The more I drank, the more I seemed to forget about the hell I was in. I didn' feel violent like my father did, I felt relieved and filled with a strange joy. It was a weird feeling, a feeling I really couldn't explain, but it had me at an unusual peace. A peace I wasn't familiar with. Suddenly I didn't wanna harm my father anymore, I just wanted to know what my mother and I had done to him that made him so angry.

I now knew the taste and effect of beer, but it was the hard liquor that turned my father into a demon. I was glad I had poured out all of my fathers whiskey because I found myself thinking about trying it too. Even though I knew what it did to him, I had this urge to prove it wasn't just the liquor, he naturally hated us. It was something hidden in the core of my family, something really bad, and knew I was the only one in the dark.

The pain in my side was getting worse, and it was getting difficult to breath. If he came home now, there was no way I could stand another attack, I would surely have to shoot him. I got up from the kitchen table and took a seat on the dining room couch. Clutching my ribs, I positioned myself on my back and turned off the TV, making sure I could hear the slightest sound. The house was quiet and calm, I could hear my heart thumping in my chest. I folded the pillow in half, and placed it under my head. It would be hours before my mother returned home from work, which meant I would have to face him alone.

I stared at the ceiling as it seemed to be spinning like a top. The beer was in charge now, and I remember thinking to myself, "I must be drunk." My hearing was fine, but my vision had doubled, I couldn't focus. I tried to sit up, hoping maybe that would help the pain in my side. I felt helpless just lying there and I didn't want him to see me in my weakness.

A couple of hours had passed and finally my worst nightmare came true. I could hear him at the front door trying to put his key in. He fumbled with lock for ten or fifteen minutes and the front door slowly opened and there he was, standing there looking like he had been beaten by his own demons. He looked weak and defeated, there was no fight left in him. A sigh of relief filled my soul as I watched him walk to his room and pass out.

I got up slowly, babysitting my injury. I took my time and quietly walked in his room to reassure myself he was asleep. He was stretched out on his stomach with his face in a pool of his last meal. I closed the bedroom door and sat back down on the couch waiting patiently for my mother to come home. Once again he had escaped death at the hands of his own son.

CHAPTER 3

The hours passed slowly while I waited for my mother to return from work. My father, still in his drunken coma, gave me the chance to gather the rest of his weapons and hide them. It was still the weekend and I knew when he woke up, the first thing he would be looking for was another drink to start the nightmare all over again.

The beer had worn off and my senses were starting to return to normal. The pain was even more severe now that I had nothing to medicate it. The beer seemed to sooth it a little and it made me wonder why my father drank so much. I didn't recall him complaining about any physical pain, but it was something about my mother he hated. What had she done? It would be years before I knew the real truth, so in the meantime the abuse continued.

I could hear him in the bedroom, snoring and grunting. He was in a deep sleep, but his rest seemed disturbed. That was the way he slept everytime he went on one of his binges, tossing and turning wildly all over the bed. I remember the times I watched him fighting and swearing at something or someone in his sleep, while I stood next to his bed trying to find the courage to kill'em.

There was a hatred in me that consumed my soul even before I knew what the word meant. The evil in my house was thick and hid behind smiling faces and material love, but the secrecy was the worst! Not being able to vent about the mess I was in ate at my soul like a hungry beast! He warned us and we obeyed him or we suffered the consequences. He always made sure we didn't mouthed a word of what went on in our house by threatening us, and we never called his bluff.

I sat quietly on the sofa watching the sun go down. He hadn't woken up yet and I prayed he'd sleep through the night, but I kept the gun close just in case. It was fully loaded with hollow point rounds, six of them, one for each chamber. I had never shot the gun before, but how hard could it be," just aim and pull the trigger," I thought to myself. I had seen him do it enough times to know it was as simple as that.

Suddenly, I heard a loud moan coming from the bedroom. The fluttering sound of sheets being thrown from the bed rang out in my ears. I sat up straight like a statue! Gripping the gun tightly in my hand, I pointed it directly at the entrance of the door. My ribs were pulsating with pain, and my breathing was fast and shallow. The adrenaline rush from the anticipation of another beating was too much for me to bear, and again I would have to face him alone.

It seemed like I'd been sitting there forever waiting for him to come rushing outta the room. I wasn't sure if he had slept long enough for the liquor to wear off, if he did I had nothing to worry about; he was a totally different person when he was sober. Briefly I entertained the thought of him being in his right mind, but he had been drunk the majority of my life and I wasn't sure if I'd recognize the difference. All I knew was I loved being around him when he was sober.

I could hear the sound of a large pair of feet landing on the hardwood floors, he was awake and I was terrified! I braced myself and stood up, and within seconds, he emerged from the room. He didn't look like the demon I'd seen before. His eyes were perily white and his skin was a smooth caramel color. His hair was stringy and long with a mixture of gray and black tint. He didn't look huge and scary the way he did when he was drunk. The hours of sleep had done justice for his appearance; but, what was he thinking?

He just stood there, looking confused, like he was trying to figure out where he was and who I was. I didn't say anything, I just gave him the space he needed to catch up with reality. He walked past me and took a seat on the recliner. Although he seemed harmless, I kept my hand on the gun, hiding it by the side of the couch cushion. I wanted to speak, but the words were only in my head, fumbling through a whirlwind of emotions. I wanted to tell him what he had done to me, but fear sealed my lips, and the only thing I could do was hope his reign of terror was over, at least for that day.

A couple of hours had gone by and neither of us had uttered a word. We were both in a mental cocoon covered by our own consciousness. We just sat there suspended in thought, not willing to make the first move. The demon in him seemed absent, he looked weak and opposed no immediate threat. For the first time that day I put aside my urge to kill him.

The jingling of keys alarmed us both as we turned toward the front door. Time had passed so rapidly, I had forgotten it was the end of my mothers work day. She turned the key and entered the house with the look of stress on her face, she was tired and drained. My father watched her as she walked past us and went into her room. I kept my eyes on him, but he maintained his silence, he didn't move, only the rotation of his head seemed alive.

I could hear my mother in the room rambling through her things, looking for something. She didn't know I had the gun, she didn't know I was hurt. I waited patiently for her to come out of the room and feed me that same lie she always did when my father beat her. "One day he's gonna wake up and we will be gone." I heard it so much, I expected it even if I knew it wasn't true.

I was emotionally scared! She wasn't the least bit concerned with what might have happened to me while she was gone She locked her bedroom door and isolated herself in her room. I was devastated! I was prepared to defend us by any means necessary and she didn't give a damn about me. My entire life had been a lie, filled with deception, and betrayal. My parents were the reality of my nightmares. Where the heart failed to exist, love showed up in money and gifts that smothered who they really were. They hid behind phony smiles and false hope, yet I trusted them.

How could love be present in the midst of so much hatred? All these thoughts invaded me while I sat just a few feet from my father. A part of me wanted to put down the gun, and reach out for his embrace. I couldn't help but wonder in his silence if he was thinking the same thing.

I didn't wanna believe she had gone to bed without checking on me. I shouldn't have been surprised, she'd done it before. I tried to understand her reasons for abandonment, but I was only eleven years old, and this was her fight, her nightmare, not mine!

Finally my father stood up, tightening his belt around his waist, he looked at me, but his look was more inviting than frightening, he was sober and I wanted to keep him that way. He looked apologetic and innocent like he was being accused of something he didn't do. I waited for him to speak, to say, " I'm sorry son," but it never came; he turned and walked out the door.

I wanted to disturb my mothers rest, I needed to tell her what happened while she was gone. Although the pain had subsided a little, I knew my ribs were broken. He was gone, and it was the perfect time for us to leave. But, she was in love with him and terrified of what he might do if she left him.

I put the gun under the couch cushion, and walked to the living room window, I had to make sure he was gone. It was the weekend, and more than likely, he was gone on another drinking binge. A sigh of relief swam over me when I didn't see his car in its usual parking space. We weren't out of the woods yet, I had to check the back because he would sometimes park in the alley when he wanted to take a drink without us knowing. I was familiar with all his tricks, it became my job to know everything about him, and I studied him every chance I got. The good and the bad in him would soon become a part of me.

I could see him from the back door window sitting in his car. He didn't appear to be drinking, he was just sitting there with his head down. I couldn't tell if he was asleep or if he was drinking, I needed to get a closer look. By the time I reached the back gate, I could see his face clearly, he was crying. I couldn't believe it, I'd never seen him cry or show any sentiment for anything. His demeanor was always cold and heartless, especially when he was drunk.

Seeing him cry should've jolted my emotions, but I felt nothing. I was becoming just like him, cold and unforgiving. I tried to force myself to approach him, talk to him, I needed some answers to his madness, an excuse, anything to explain his behavior. But, fear of acceptance was holding me back. The thought of him rejecting me would be more than I could stand. I needed to face my fear, so I stepped out on faith.

I opened the gate and got in the car on the passenger side. He didn't even react to my presence, he just continued crying. Suddenly he wasn't that demon anymore; he was a weak and defeated vessel who had been victimized by his own pity. I sat beside him quietly and allowed him to take it all in.

We sat in the car for hours in total silence, neither one of us spoke a word. Strangely, it felt like we were bonding, but without effort, it was just automatically happening. It was a good feeling, a feeling I never got the chance to get used to. I wasn't sure if I could trust it, it wasn't the first time I'd seen him sober, we had been down that road many times.

It made me think about the times he would plan hunting and fishing trips. I was only nine years old when he bought me my first weapon, it was a twenty gauge pump shotgun. I was the happiest kid alive. I remember thinking, "I'm gonna finally get a chance to kill something."

The memories were short lived, as reality came rushing back to the situation I was currently in. Just as I was about to confront him, he opened the car door and got out. In an instant my fear resurfaced. He opened the gate and headed for the house.

The beer had worn completely off and the pain in my side was coming alive, no longer numb from intoxication, I was sober just like him. I opened the car door and got out slowly, clutching my side. I wanted him to see me in pain, maybe it would make him think about the way he treated us. Maybe he would even consider stopping. It was a long shot, but I always prayed for those results.

My mother was sound asleep, and she had no idea what was headed her way. He was only a few feet from her and I was in too much pain to run and catch up with him. By the time I made it to the steps, he was already in the house. I pushed the door open slowly. I really didn' know what state of mind he was in, so I didn't want him to think I was sneaking up on him. I closed the door behind me, and took a seat at the kitchen table. I had to get to the gun before it crossed his mind.

The bedroom door to my mothers room was still closed, and the house was quiet. I picked up a bottle of aspirin my mother had left on the kitchen table and took a couple and opened the fridge to grab a beer to wash them down. Once again, the cold bitter taste lit up my taste buds and I was popping them open one after another.

It didn't take long for the effect of the beer to kick in. The more I drank, the more brave I became. I was ready to face him, there was no more running.

The empty cans were lined up on the table, I stared at them as my eyesight began to double. I was drunk, I looked just like him. My thoughts were scrambled, and my legs felt like silly putty as I tried to stand up and walk toward the dining room where he was. The walls were closing in, and the floor was swaying back and forth. I drank way too much.

One step at a time, I managed to make it to the couch. My father was sitting calmly in his recliner with his feet elevated. His eyes were closed, but he wasn't asleep. He seemed to be meditating or maybe planning something secretly to himself. My undeveloped mind didn't grant me the opportunity to figure him out, so I just kept quiet, hoping he would say or do something that would unveil his thoughts. He was a master at concealing his attacks.

They came like a sudden storm, moving everything in its way! It was the face of the devil for an eleven year old, and a nightmare for my mother.

The silence was becoming unbearable, I had to say something. I turned to look at him, it was now or never. I stood up, and pulled up my shirt exposing the huge purple and black bruise on my side. The beer had moved swiftly through my system, causing me to lean back and forth, the room spinning, my stomach boiling. Finally the words found their way to the tip of my tongue; "Daddy, daddy, look at me, look at what you did." He lifted his head, and said, "let me see that, how did that happen, what do you mean, look at what you did." I couldn't believe it, he didn't have a clue, he denied it all. He didn't remember any of it. He didn't even remember being drunk.

I was furious! Not only did he beat me, he lied about it. My face wet with tears, my emotions spiralled outta control, I was a mental wreck! I tried to pull myself together, but the beer only enhanced wha I was feeling. I was drunk, and now the porcelain god was calling me.

The sickness was taking charge, and everything I'd previously eaten was climbing up the funnel of my throat. The awful mixture of food invaded my taste buds as it came pouring out of my mouth accompanied by a horrible stench.

Somehow I made it to the bathroom, and found myself in the same position I'd seen my father in so many times, my arms wrapped around the porcelain god, praying for relief. It was crazy! I was sick as hell, but I loved the taste, and that was the moment I knew I would drink it every chance I got.

CHAPTER 4

For the first time in my life I realized I was becoming just like him, a fucking lush. I liked the way the beer tasted, I couldn't deny it. I even smelled like him, it was coming out my pores, I was sweating and little beads of water ran down my face. Vomit was all over the toilet seat and floor, the bathroom was a mess and so was I. I was on my knees. Praying to an idol god just like him. I was so drunk, I'd forgotten all about the injury to my ribs.

An hour or so had passed by before I was able to get up and clean myself up. My mother had left for work without any confrontation from my father; she had escaped another fight. My father was asleep on the dining room sofa, so I decided not to disturb him. The longer he stayed sober, the better off we were. Our house hadn't known serenity often, so I took advantage of it.

It was a Saturday morning and normally I would be planning a day with my friends. But, this particular saturday was different, I had found a new friend, and all I needed to do was wait for my mother to restock the fridge. It was definitely in need since I had drank damn near every can she had, and I knew it would be the first thing she would be looking for when she got home. You see, she was an alcoholic too, I just didn't know it yet because she wasn't violent like my father. She could finish a 24 can case of budweiser so fast you would think it was only a six pack. But, the part that amazed me was, she never seemed to be drunk. I never saw her stumble or stagger, trip or fall, or even vomit. It was like water flowing through her body, it had no affect on her. She was the coolest lush I knew.

After cleaning myself up that morning I went in my room and laid down, watching the room spin while I waited for the effect of the beer to wear off. The getting sick part was gonna take some getting used to, it was a horrible feeling. How my father tolerated it all those years, I will never know.

The entire day had passed me by, and the sun was beginning to set. My father was still asleep on the sofa and I was still drunk. I hadn't anticipated it lasting this long, and the only good thing that came from it was it stopped the pain; I guess I was too wasted to notice it.

I could hear my father grunting in the dining room as he woke from a deep sleep. His feet hit the floor with authority, followed by a long breath of much needed rest that startled me out of my drunken state. I tried to sit up, fighting against the liquid consumption in my body, but it was no use, my limbs were weak, and feeble. The beer was still in charge, and my father was sober and at his best self.

I could hear him walking around in the house, and then it dawned on me; the gun was under the couch cushion. I needed to get up and get it before he found it, but I didn't have the strength. I had hid the rest of his guns and it was only a matter of time before he missed them. He wouldn't be much of a threat while he was sober, but I didn't wanna take any chances, so I forced myself outta the bed, legs wiggly, I had to get to that gun.

Somehow I managed to stand up and balance myself, it wasn't perfect, but at least I wasn't rocking back and forth. Briefly, in that moment, I remembered wanting to be like my father. Not the father that beat us, but the one that took me hunting, fishing, the one that bought me my first motorcycle, the one that paid the bills, the one that went to work everyday, that was the one I idolized. But, now that man was long gone, lost in the bottom of a whiskey bottle. He was the devil in the flesh, and I hadn't fully taken it in yet, but I was his trainee.

One step at a time, I made my way into the dining room where he was, standing in front of the tv adjusting the channels. The couch didn't look disturbed, so I knew he hadn't found the gun. He looked at me as though he was trying to figure me out. He looked totally different when he was sober. His skin was a smooth and even carmel color, his eyes a glossy white, and his hair was brushed backward in a neat ponytail; it was a clever disguise. He continued scanning through the channels and ignored my presence.

My father never did apologize that day for the beating he gave me. I missed six months of school because of broken ribs. Each year his drinking got worse and so did the abuse. My mother was drinking more and so was I. HELL, we were all alcoholics, trapped in a world of shit!

No one outside of my house knew what I was going through, I wanted to tell someone, but I was too afraid. I was in high school now, and my father had retired from his job, which meant he was home everyday. We had to fight for our lives every fucking day!

The basement became my sanctuary. It was where I'd go to get away from all the confusion in my life. I had started snorting cocaine and smoking weed, but no one knew except a couple of my friends. The drugs numbed me and made me forget about the drama. The more I used, the further away the pain went, and I tried to keep it as far away as possible.

I had never known my father to do anything but drink, but I had graduated above that, I was in the big leagues, I was doing grown man shit, the cool shit, the shit that made me feel like I was king, and nothing could touch me.

I didn't have a habit, I mean, I wasn't stealing for it or committing crime or doing any crazy shit to get it, I just did it to loosen up, relax, clear my head and the weed helped me stay balanced since the cocaine was an upper. I did it everyday, but no one could tell, I always made sure I had some weed to keep me calm. It wasn't long before I stopped drinking, I got tired of getting sick and vomiting all over myself, it wasn't cool. It smelled bad and it didn't look good in front of the ladies.

I was in the 10th grade now and my sister thought it would be a good idea if I'd move in with her, so I did. I had my own devil now, but I hadn't met him yet. He was growing inside me one minute at a time. He had followed me, waiting patiently for me to feed him, and nourish him. He had plans to destroy me, to obliterate my dreams, to wipe out any chance of success in my life. He was smooth and calculating, I had no idea he was there, I had no premonition of his presence. He was attached to me like the skin on my bones. He was a part of me, like a twin that had been born bonded to my side. He was quiet and skillful, but somehow his voice spoke to me. I wasn't dumb, I know God wouldn't tell me to snort cocaine, but still I obeyed hm. I was his student, and he had been secretly teaching me all of life.

I remember the first time I met the devil, I was around 19 years old. He wasn't at all what people said he was, he didn't have red skin, long fangs, horns on his head, a long pointed tail or pitchfork in his hand. He was a powdery white substance mixed with baking soda and water, boiled over an open flame transforming it into "crack cocaine." He was my master, and I was his slave. He was a tiny white pebble with unbelievable power! He didn't have eyes, a nose, a mouth , or limbs. He just teamed up with a glass pipe, waited for me to set fire to him, and fucked up my life!

At first, he was cunning, he made me trust him by using the drugs to rescue me from my self pity. Every hit I took gave me this false peace that only lasted a few seconds, and then I found myself chasing that hit over and over again, trying to find that peace again. In the midst of that short lived moment I was in paradise, all of my present pain wiped away. Snorting it never gave me that serenity, I was hooked! If only I'd known where it was leading me.

CHAPTER 5

Smoking the drug was nothing like snorting it, it packed a much more powerful punch when it was on that pipe. But I wasn't alone, he was destroying lives all over my neighborhood. Almost everybody I knew was getting hooked on it. We were all consumed by a mental cloud of madness orchestrated by the devil himself. The high was intense and demanding. Once you started, you couldn't stop, even if you ran outta money you had to find ways to get more.

I managed to clean myself up with the help of my first six month inpatient treatment facility. I learned a few things while I was there to help me cope with the outside world, but somehow I knew they would be no match for the demon inside me. He was much too powerful for a few rules written in a book. And besides," if this treatment was so effective, why were there so many people fucked up." My neighborhood was full of people walking around like zombies, their pupils dilated like they had seen a ghost, sweating, and looking malnourished, like they hadn't eaten in weeks.

The demon hadn't beaten me down yet, I still had my composure, or at least I thought I did. I didn't even notice what it had done to me until I cleaned up, and by the time I figured it out, I was ready for another hit.

The second time around was nothing like the first. The drug was much more aggressive! The high was much more potent, and the feeling was incredible! I knew from that very first hit I had found my best friend. The devil had me and there wasn't a damn thing I could do about it. That's when the journey began. That was the day I descended into HELL!

The flames were all around me, but I had yet to get burned. I was in hell and didn't even know it. It might sound crazy, but I was having fun getting high. The devil was a smooth operator. He had a way of glamorizing evil, he could make wrong look so right I didn't even think twice before I reacted.

The high took me to a place of indescribable pleasure. I went to a place where pain, trails, and tribulations didn't exist. My father's devil was his now, I didn't have to be subject to his abuse anymore. My basement sanctuary wasn't needed anymore, I found a new place to hide, in a cloud of white smoke.

I had graduated from high school the previous year, and moved back home. I was a man now and I wasn't taking anymore shit from my father. To my surprise, things had changed. He wasn't drinking anymore, he was sober, and had been for a while. At first I didn't trust it, I thought it was just another one of his tricks. My mother seemed happier and the house was peaceful. It had been a long time since my father and I had a "normal" conversation, and because of his drinking I'd forgotten how to communicate.

I was in college now, so I did most of my partying on the weekends. My sister had high expectations for my life and I was trying hard not to let her down. My habit was progressing, and my desire for the drug was becoming more and more difficult to control. I couldn't hide it anymore, my appearance gave me away. The devil had taken complete control, and I was in a nightmare with my eyes wide open that would last almost 25 years.

It was like I had fallen asleep with my eyes open. I could see everything happening to me, but I was powerless over it. It was like a night terror, but more real than anyone could ever imagine. The effects of the high made every part of my body tingle, it was better than sex! It was nothing like my father's habit, I wasn't falling all over the place, tripping over my own feet. It was euphoric, and intensifying. But it came with an evil not known to man. An evil that invited me in with a welcome so cunning and baffling I didn't even see it coming.

The alcohol had done its damage to my parents marriage, and after 40 years, they decided to go their separate ways. I moved to Memphis with my father where I spent 5 outta 9 years getting high before he died in 2003 of a brain stroke that landed me back on the streets of Chicago homeless. That was when the devil started to tear me limb from limb.

CHAPTER 6

The winters were cold and brutal. The strong winds whipped through the broken windows of the abandoned building with vengeance! There was nowhere to hide from the huge snowflakes that covered the floors. This was one of many places in the neighborhood I had claimed as my home. Some had running water and electricity, some didn't. Nevertheless, they were all shelter to me. I brought in old bedding people had thrown away for my comfort. Old blankets, sheets, and clothes, anything I could find to keep me warm late night walking through the alleys.

This was 63rd street, a neighborhood under siege by the devil's soldiers, the drug dealers. There was no escaping the chemical madness, it was everywhere! The crack rock was in charge, it was the new sheriff in town.

Every morning I got up to start my day, the craving for crack woke up with me. It would be the first thing on my agenda no matter what condition I was in. The 711 convenience store was how I financed my morning hit I called, "a wakeup," I stood there for hours, begging for change until I had enough for my medicine. Once I got that first hit, it was off to the races.

I ran all day. The drug pimped me like a two dollar whore, working me from sunup to sun down. One 10 dollar bag at a time, it was consistent insanity, it was my job to feed my demon daily without ceasing.

I went days without eating, the crack provided my nourishment. My body depended on it, it called me like a mother beckoning for her child. My thoughts knew nothing else, my mind had been captured and weakened by the power of the tiny pebble. It was a spiritual battle and the God in me was losing badly.

I remember saying, "I will never be like my father," but I was worse than him. I was homeless, living on the streets and sometimes, finding my meals in garbage cans. I was at my lowest, but my will to change was not in me, I loved the high more than I hated the misery.

The bad times disguised themselves as good times, therefore blinding me from every evil that lurked in the confines of my polluted thinking. My inner man had been barricaded, while my flesh went on a ride of total self- destruction.

It was Armageddon in the world I lived in, trapped inside of a cocoon of crushed hope, misplaced dreams; a world of forgotten expectations and gifts from God carelessly tossed aside. I was a picture painted perfect, but a talent wasted by a decision birth from the gift of free will. Yes, I was in deep! So deep, I couldn't see past the cloud of smoke that escaped my lungs after every hit. It was my destiny, and I needed to go there every second of my life, nothing else mattered!

63rd street was hell above ground! Every block was engulfed with the flames of addiction to drugs in one form or another. The alleys and abandoned buildings were occupied with lost souls such as myself, searching for the next high, trying to escape the reality of a lifestyle chosen with no meaning. A lost people trying to recapture a mind scattered in a field of distant memories of who they used to be.

It was all so surreal, no family, I was all alone, caught up in a complete mess of confusion. I held on tightly to my best friend, my glass pipe. It was the only temporary escape from the mental condition that plagued my mind. It was my very short lived freedom I needed constantly to stay sane. I carried it with me everywhere I went, it was a part of me, it was the most important part of my existence next to my drug of choice, and I wore it with no shame. I was a dopefiend with a degree in nothing.

I had succeeded at doing absolutely nothing with my life and I somehow managed to keep a smile on my face here and there, It was the only way I kept from going completely insane.

I could feel the spirit of God trying to fight its way to the surface, but the demon in me was stronger than my will to change. I was a madman on a strange quest of destruction, guided by something sinister, something much more evil than my father, something I couldn't kill with a gun, something I couldn't see. It was like a bad dream that lasted forever.

And then it dawned on me; it was the devil, yet in another form. Not like he was when I saw him with my father, but different. He brought a brief sense of peace with him in the form of a small piece of crack. As long as I nourished his hunger, he gave me serenity. As long as I was high, I didn't have a problem in the world. It didn't matter if I hadn't taken a bath in weeks, or brushed my teeth in days, or changed clothes in a week or two, it wasn't a priority. My only concern was my next hit, it was always at the top of my to do list.

The nights on 63rd street were always the worst. The bitter cold winter evenings were devastating for me. Most of the people I got high with had somewhere to go once the drugs were all gone. I was always the one left searching for shelter for the night. Sometimes in an abandoned building, a hallway, someone's garage, a dumpster, in an alley, or just curled up on the sidewalk under some cardboard boxes; how I woke up the next morning without frostbite, still baffles me to this day.

I remember some nights under the back porch of an abandoned house on 61st and kedzie, I cleaned out a little cozy spot for me to sleep. It was the middle of the winter, and the wind was wicked and viciously cold. I had a couple of old worn out comforters I'd found in the garbage can to battle the blistering weather. I crawled in under the porch , and settled in for the night, tucking the blankets under each side of me. The snow was blowing aggressively on top of me, but I was well covered.

The tears started to fill my eyes as I thought about my family. I was sober, the reality of my situation hit me for the first time. I was alone, nobody gave a damn about me, nobody but my new best friend. I opened my mouth and spit out two small bags of crack. I opened them both and stuffed them on my pipe. I struck my lighter and put the flame to the tiny pebbles and watched them as they started to melt. The white smoke rushed down the funnel of the glass pipe and entered my body with authority! Within seconds, my entire body relaxed in a blissful peace. My mind surrendered all that haunted my conscience. But a side of me wanted to die, aside of me needed to be set free from this demon. But all I could do was pray that it would be the last time I opened my eyes.

I wanted to see heaven. I had read about it enough to know it wasn't here. I don't even remember going to sleep that night, but I do remember asking God to take my life. I didn't wanna wake up to that madness no more. It wasn't until I opened my eyes that morning and realized I was still in a world of shit, that the devil answers prayers to.

I was shaking and covered in snow, my hands frozen to the concrete slab beneath me. The pain from the cold weather surged through my bones like electricity. I wanted to free my hands, but I was afraid I would break my fingers. My hands were inside my gloves, but they felt naked against the blistering cold. I tried to sit up, but I couldn't move, my entire body was bonded to concrete beneath me. I knew if I didn't break free, I would soon freeze to death. "Maybe this is the way my prayer for death will be answered," I thought to myself.

I dismissed any further opportunity to rid myself of the immediate danger I was in. This was my chance to beat the devil at his own game and take my own life. He was killing me slowly, but tonight that would all end, I was in charge now, and the morning would tell a different story, the nightmare would be over, and I would be with God.

CHAPTER 7

I laid still in the below zero weather. I was determined to end my life. I dreaded chasing the high one more day. The cold was brutal, and mean; I tried hard to block it out, but the wind kept pushing the snow against my body like a huge shovel. "There was no way I'd survive another night of these conditions," I thought to myself.

I tried to sleep, hoping I wouldn't wake up. But suicide was not an accomplice of my self-destructive thinking, I couldn't fall asleep. I tore my frozen body from the ice beneath me, tossing the snow covered blankets aside, I stood erect. It felt like my entire body was frost bitten.

The devil had his unique way of making me feel like the lowest creature on earth. Even in conditions such as these, he managed to find a way to reel me right back in.

My hands and feet were numb, I couldn't feel a thing! I climbed the stairs that led to my little cubby hole, one step at a time. The bright morning sun blinded me momentarily, as I raised my frozen hands to block the warm rays. It was the beginning of a new day, a chance for me to do something different with my life. I was sober, the same way I'd be every morning I faced a new day. The thought of sobriety was always there, but it was just that, a thought. The weakness in me always prevailed, and before I knew it I was somewhere taking that first hit, waking up that demon all over again.

The dunkin donuts across the alley from my hell under the porch was my temporary salvation. It was where I'd go most mornings to get warm after fighting the cold weather under the porch all night. The staff that worked there had gotten familiar with me, and they let me sit at one of the tables against the wall as long as I didn't bother the customers.

I didn't know it at the time, but now I believe it was God putting people in my path to help me. But back then, the devil's love potion (crack) was everything to me. It was the answer to all the pain and misery in my life. I accepted it, I embraced it, I held it by the hand like it was my own child, and I defended it against anything and anyone who got in its way!

I slept for 4 or 5 hours that morning in dunkin donuts. I woke up warm and thawed out, but my clothes were a little damp from the snow and ice melting from the fabric. The depression started setting in immediately, I knew what the day would bring, it was time to start the chase all over again'

The first hit of the day was usually the easiest. It didn't take much effort, the drug dealers were waiting to get you started, it as an investment for them. The quicker they got you high, the more money they would make. They knew once you got that first hit, you would chase that shit all day.

That was the life I had chosen for myself, or should I say, "my parents chose for me." Either way, I was fucked! I was in it up to my neck, and I was absolutely convinced it was how I was gonna die, strung out on drugs.

I hadn't eaten anything in a week, but that didn't matter. As soon as I got that first one in me, food wouldn't even be an option.

I was well rested and ready to tackle the pending situations, whatever challenge came my way. The crack had shaped me into a survivor under the worst conditions. There was nothing I couldn't conquer with my glass friend, together we were unstoppable!

The more I fed my demon, the stronger he became. I was attentive to his voice, as he called out to me from the depths of my soul. I followed him into some of the darkest places, seeking out his instruction, not considering the consequences. He was my god, and I was his student with perfect attendance.

He pushed away the wind from my ears, as he spoke to me that cold afternoon leaving Dunkin donuts. I was sober, and yet he troubled my spirit. I couldn't dismiss him, my mind was his, and so my body followed. He was no longer a mystery, his evil was present and he made me love it.

His voice was audible now. I could hear it just as I could hear myself speak. He was leading me that winter afternoon, and I knew it. Before I realized where I was, I found myself standing in front of 711 begging for change, something I hated doing, but the devil made me feel no shame.

That's the way it started everyday, that first one. If only I could've resisted that first one. It was like that first drink. I saw my father many times sober, but once he took that first drink, he didn't stop until he passed out. But now in a similar way I knew his fight, his struggle, I could identify with his worthlessness. He was a man to most that knew him, but to me he was weak and I had become something much worse.

It didn't take long for me to hustle the fee for my daily dose of misery. The devil didn't waste time providing destruction, he was always prompt when it came to that. For a crack addict, 10 dollars was like hitting the lottery, if you had enough for a rock, you had the winning ticket. Well, that morning, like most, I got my chance to cash in my winning ticket. I made the ten dollars so fast, I had forgotten all about how cold it was.

Once I got my hand on that drug, that's all I cared about. For those brief minutes of substance abuse, nothing could touch me, I was invincible. Life only existed to quench my craving. The hustle, the preparation, watching the pipe fill up with smoke was all a part of my sick need to escape reality. I chased it, one bag at a time, I had to keep it going or face emotions I had no control over.

At this point, being sober was much worse than being high. Without the aid of the devil's love potion, the depression would be overwhelming. A sane mind was not an option in this lifestyle. Trying to battle the horrors of addition was a fight fueled by insanity. It always took you further than you wanted to go, kept you longer than you wanted to stay, and cost you more than you willing to pay. You never knew what it would influence you to do next.

I walked the streets for hours after that first morning hit. Pupils dilated, eyes wide open like I'd seen a ghost. The paranoia was intense, everybody and everything looked suspect. People looked at me and shook their heads in pity, a young man trapped in the darkest corners of his own mind.

There was no basement anymore for my sanctuary, no place to hide from the pity that judged me after the high wore off. The thought of who I used to be was a distant memory in which I had no strength to recall that person. The dumpsters in the alleys became my new sanctuaries. I selected them carefully in secluded spots where no one could see me. I made sure they were empty, and then I climbed in, closed the top and sat there in total darkness, sometimes for hours, sometimes just to get high, sometimes all night. It was rock bottom for me, the lowest of the lowest. I had lost my mind, and didn't even know it.

Many nights I hid in those cold steel dumpsters having conversations with myself. Trying to convince myself I wasn't going crazy, or hadn't gone crazy. Trying to figure out how I got there, how did my choices lead to this? Questioning myself over and over again, hoping for an answer from me when I'm the one responsible.

Talking to myself became a habit, I did it mostly when the high came down. It was the only time my mind allowed my conscious to release some of the hell I was in. The more the high came down, the more depressed I was. Being sober made me face the reality of how I was living. The devil hated me, and he made me pay every time I tried not to take that first hit. The abandonment of my family was his greatest weapon, and he used it every time I thought about denying him.

It was the free highs that did the worst damage. The high that came from nowhere when you didn't have any money. The crack that was given to you by drug dealers and so-called friends who wanted to keep you in that circle of confusion. I was always a victim of the free high. I made sure I always had something free coming from every drug dealer in the neighborhood every day. I worked for them faithfully, earning the free crack that kept me in bondage with every bag I smoked. I knew my life was a mess, but I didn't care, I loved the high, it was the only thing that made me feel good.

I sold crack for the dealers like I was one of them. Sometimes I even made a little money on the side, but it never did me any good, I'd only spend it on drugs. Sometimes I ran off with the drugs, risking my life, knowing I could get beat really bad or maybe even killed. I never considered the consequences, as long as I had the drugs, nothing else mattered. I had invested years in this madness, and I didn't know if I would ever find my way back. I was highly medicated, and outta my rabbit ass mind, and at this point restoration wasn't looking too good.

CHAPTER 8

Yes, I was finally there. I had made it. That place I'd heard them talk about when I was in that treatment facility. That place most addicts find themselves sooner or later during the course of their active use, rock bottom. This was a place that most of us as addicts feared, but somehow we strangely welcomed it. We never intended to dig the hole that buried us so deep in the shit, it just happened, one hit at a time.

I was a zombie, walking up and down the alleys and streets day and night searching for that next hit, it was my job and I punched that clock everyday faithfully. But this day wasn't like the rest, I knew from the very first moment I took that first hit, something terrible was gonna happen that day.

I had just left one of my usual spots behind the dumpster in the alley where I took most of my morning fixes. It was usually before the kids were out headed for school and the early morning traffic of people going to work, it was quiet, no distractions.

The dumpster was behind walgreens, it was a meeting spot for a lot of us that were in captivity by the devil's love potion. It was something to see, a bunch of lost souls smoking crack in broad daylight like it was legal. We were the outcast of the neighborhood, nobody respected us and nobody gave a damn about us.

I came out of the alley that morning on cloud nine. That first hit had me wired! Everything was moving fast, and it seemed like everybody knew I was high. I sat down on the concrete slab by the bus stop like I did every morning, and waited on Jenny. It was cold, but the unshaded space allowed the warm rays of sun to blanket the area I was sitting in.

Usually Jenny would meet me there every morning like clock work. We put our money together and purchase our fix. Jenny was a slim white girl who made her money mostly by prostitution. The women in the neighborhood that were on drugs lived a hard life. They sold their bodies for five and ten dollars all day just to feed that demon that controlled them. A lot of them were homeless just like me, living in abandoned buildings and eating outta garbage cans. Some had even lost their lives in the madness that came with the lifestyle.

The longer I sat there, the more my stomach began to sour. It was a feeling of emptiness. Jenny was a no show. I didn't know what to think, but the circumstances of our lifestyles didn't leave much room for denial. I knew in this life when someone didn't show, they were either in jail or dead.

It didn't take long for the news to spread throughout the neighborhood that Jenny had been found in the park dead with her throat slashed from ear to ear.

Crack was medicine for pain, all pain. Even the sting of death had no effect on me. The devil's love potion was a weapon of mass destruction against anything and anyone that got in its way. I thought I'd seen hell in my house growing up. But it was nothing compared to what I was living in the streets. My father's drinking was a walk in the park next to the horror of crack cocaine. Crack ruled every aspect of my life. I had no control over my body or my mind, and I did exactly what it told me to do, no exceptions!

After Jenny's death I went into isolation. Jenny was an addict like me, but she was my friend. She was one of the people I got high with I actually cared about.

I spent the next five days on a suicide mission. I smoked and smoked without eating or sleeping, trying to end it all. I prayed for death with every hit I took, as my heart raced rapidly from the powerful substance. I wanted the peace that Jenny had, but the devil wouldn't give it to me. I hated my life, I wanted to die, but I loved the high. I was messed up! Caught between the consequences of reality and the confusion of love.

That wasn't my first week on a binge, I'd done it plenty of times. They all ended the same, me somewhere dirty, smelly, digging in somebody's garbage looking for something to eat or passing out wherever my body shuts down. Sometimes I would smoke so much crack, I would pass out in some of the strangest places and wake up, not knowing how I got there. Sometimes in abandoned buildings unfamiliar to me, on sidewalks in neighborhoods unknown to me, and alleys I've never been in before. Sometimes I even ended up in jail for crimes I'd committed to support my habit.

The neighborhood was kinda quiet the day Jenny got killed. It was cold and the usual activity of drug dealers and addicts were at a minimum because of all of the police prowling the area investigating Jenny's death. The devil had been busy that year, Jenny was the third person whom I had known that had died in the grips of the glass pipe. There was no escaping him, I had accepted it. I was an addict, and nothing would change that, not even God.

63rd street was like a graveyard for the undead to me. A place where drug addicts followed an illusion of false hope and misplaced love in a man made substance called, "crack." It took me seven years to find my plot there after leaving Memphis. After my mother's death in 1996 I was on my quest for a final resting place. And to top it off, my father passed away in 2003, just three months before I moved back to Chicago.

I blamed everybody for the mess I was in. Especially my mom and dad who exposed me to all the abuse during my childhood. All the lies they told, all the promises they made. I even blamed the people in the neighborhood who introduced me to the drug. But, most of all I blamed God, where was he, I was his child, his creation, and now the devil had claimed my soul. I was in the prime of my life, with all of my dreams at my fingertips, but I couldn't grasp them, didn't want them, they weren't important anymore, the high was KING, everything else was irrelevant. I was a puppet, dangling from strings of smoke, and despite all the misery that came with it, I was having fun destroying my life.

As long as I stayed high, the reality of my situation didn't bother me. It was getting dark, the sun was setting and the temperature was dropping. I hated the night, that meant I would have to find somewhere to sleep. That was the routine everyday, hustle up the money, get high, hustle again, get high, keep going, keep going, and going, and going, until you just couldn't go anymore. By the time the day ended, I was exhausted, and sometimes my body would shut down right where I stood.

I made my way back to my cubby hole under the porch to settle in for the night. The hustle was slow, it was bitter cold and there was not much traffic in and out of 711. I was sober. I hated being sober. It made all the shit I was going through surface all at once. Every painful memory, all the years of my life wasted on drugs, it all came rushing back. These were the times I prayed for death! These were the times I needed my mom the most. But, she had done what she'd always done, she lied to me, she died and left me here to face this shit alone.

I remember feeling like I was in prison, and my sentence was life on drugs without the possibility of parole. I was being judged by the devil, not God. Every time I hit that pipe the evil whispers mentally drove me to the edge of insanity, just enough to keep me from falling completely over.

I laid still under the old blankets trying to stay warm as the night air prepared to punish me as it did every night I resided there. It was home now that most of the abandoned buildings in the neighborhood had been boarded up. The dumpsters were off limits since I almost got dumped in the back of a garbage truck after falling asleep in one of them. That was the weird thing about crack, it made you do some crazy shit!

For the first time in a long time I was sober, I was thinking clearly, well almost clearly. I imagined my life without drugs. A house, a wife, a family, a job, all the beautiful things that life has to offer. I wanted those things just like any other "normal person." And just as quickly as the thought came, it was gone; and before I knew it, I was up and on my feet. The hunt was on for that next hit!

It was 2 in the morning, windy and cold. It started to snow, and the devil had summoned me out of my shelter for his love potion. I was on a mission by him and by any means necessary I had to feed my demons. The streets were clear, there was not a soul to see in the blistering cold. I had no idea where my next hit would come from, but I had to have it, the guilt was overwhelming. I couldn't stop thinking about Jenny as I fought my way through the blowing snow. She was free from this life of misery, I wished it had been me. I welcomed death but the grave didn't want me.

The wind was vicious as I turned my back toward it, trying to keep the snow out of my face. I was sober and my body was starting to crave food. I hadn't eaten anything in 5 or 6 days and I didn't have any money, so my only option would be to find something in one of the dumpsters behind burger king or dunkin donuts. I decided to look for food before I got high. If I got high before I ate, the crack would be my food.

My body was used to substituting the food for drugs, it was something I'd done for years. But sometimes after going without eating, I had to eat or my blood sugar would drop so low I would pass out.

Dunkin Donuts was always my first choice. They were open 24 hours and I knew at 10 pm every night they threw away all the donuts they didn;t sell that day.

It was a five block walk from where I was to dunkin donuts. Without the drugs in my system, the reality of my situation was upfront and personal. By the time I made it to the dumpster behind dunkin donuts, my hands were so cold I couldn't feel my fingertips.

I lifted the top on the dumpster and there they were, garbage bags full of donuts. I reached in and grabbed two, they were heavy, and I had a long way to go in the aggressive weather.

It was a long walk back to the cubby hole and I still hadn't got that last hit I needed. With no money that late it didn't seem possible. Somehow, some way I knew the devil wouldn't let me down, he had a way of making sure he kept me medicated. Just as I crossed the alley at 63st behind the electronic store, there it was, laying right there in the snow, a roll of money in a rubber band. I dropped the donuts, and picked it up. I couldn't believe it. I ran in the alley and squatted down between two dumpsters and counted it. $400, "damn, here we go again," I said to myself.

The sad part about it was, I didn't even think about buying anything I needed, like clothes, underwear, soap, toothpaste, food, or maybe renting a room so I could take a hot shower. Nope, the only thing on my mind was crack,I was gonna spend every dollar on it and I knew it.

I stuffed the money in my pocket and tiptoed through the wet snow down the alley hoping no one saw me. It was party time and I didn't have to share with anyone. I was sure that would be the final episode of my life, $400 worth, there was no way my heart would survive that.

The streets were clear, not a drug dealer in sight. I didn't consider, maybe it could be God giving me a chance to make better choices. Instead, I just fought my way through the snow to my cubby hole, wrapped myself up in my old blankets and waited patiently for the morning to come, when all the crack I wanted would be at my fingertips. Now I wish I had my donuts. But there was no way I was walking back to get them. The anticipation of the morning high was good enough.

I didn't know it back then, but that is the tricky thing about crack, it has a way of messing with the mind. It is a psychological high, a mental addiction. It has a way of talking to you,and a way of making you listen. That's what makes it compatible with the devil, it whispers evil and then it withdraws from it's whispers to watch the destruction. It comes to steal, kill, and destroy, all the character traits of the devil.

I tried to sleep, but the bitter cold was just too much when I was sober. Lucky for me I was well dressed for the single digit weather that night. I only had about 4 hours to wait before the sun would be up and my wait would be over. With that much money it would probably last me a day or two if I didn't get free hearted and start sharing it.

The paranoia from a crack high could get real intense, sometimes getting high by myself wasn't a good idea. With all the money I had, I probably needed to find somebody to smoke with.

With Jenny not around anymore I only had a couple of other people I could trust; my buddy Shorty and my girl Janice. They were just like me, homeless and dedicated to the lifestyle. They were both hardcore addicts who did whatever it took to feed their demons. We were like the three blind mice, neither one of us couldn't see past the end of a glass pipe.

After making it through the night, I got up, wrapped up my blankets and headed out to get my medicine. It had been a long time since I got my hands on that much money all at once. $400, it was like winning the lottery.

The drug dealers were out early that morning. I flagged down the first one I saw. I didn't tease myself like I would usually do, buying one bag at a time. I spent the whole $400 all at once. I wanted to make sure I smoked enough to make my heart explode in my chest! I changed my mind, I wasn't sharing shit!

I bought my crack and looked for an empty dumpster to get high in. I wanted to make sure I wasn't disturbed and I wanted to be good and dead by the time someone found my body. I walked down the alley just a couple of blocks from where I'd found the money and climbed in the first empty one I saw. It was cold as hell, and dark. I opened the plastic bag and broke a piece of the huge rock and stuffed it on my pipe. It was my first hit of the day, it took effect immediately, rushing my system like a storm! The deceitful sensation of the drug warmed my body like a smooth summer breeze as I relaxed and prepared for the second coming. All of my problems, pain, guilt, pity, and worthlessness glided down the glass pipe into a white cloud, vaporizing into the thin air. I was free, if only for a short while, I was free.

I sat still in the dumpster, captivated by the high. The crack was pure and powerful! My heart was beating fast, very fast! I wanted to end it, but now I wasn't so sure. I mean, I wanted to die, but I didn't wanna suffer. I sat the pipe between my legs and tried to calm myself, but the rock had control. And just as quickly as it all started, it stopped. Once again the devil had cheated me outta death. I reached down, picked up the pipe and loaded it again.

He wouldn't let me die. No matter how much I smoked, somehow my body sustained it like a seasoned vet. For a moment I thought, "maybe it's God sparing my life." But then that didn't make sense to me. Why would Gould God watch me suffer like this.

I put the flame to the pipe for the second time. The effect from the first hit hadn't completely worn off yet when the drug hit my system for a second time. The second hit was so powerful, I blew out the flame, dropped the pipe and pushed the lid open to the dumpster. I wanted to climb out, but the crack had me so paranoid, I just knew somebody was standing there, waiting for me to come out. There I was, spooked, frooze, unable to move, sitting in a dumpster in broad daylight in an alley with the lid wide open and scared shitless! Yes, this was definitely the devil's work. He had already managed to destroy my life, and now he had driven me insane.

My mind was gone! I sat in that dumpster until dark, smoking hit after hit. The more I smoked, the more paranoid I became. I was so high, at times I even thought I saw people looking in on me. I could even hear whispering on the outside.

I had fallen in love with the wrong thing, guided by the wrong god. Led by an entity of many voices and faces. I was a faithful servant to an unseen force that had me in a surreal reality of no return.

The reality of my situation was real! I was garbage. I was much worse than the man I vowed never to become, my father. The abandonment of my own soul was too much to recapture. My visions for a better life were blinded by the chemical madness of a man made substance. Yes, it was the end, just not the end I expected. I was suffering, and the devil intended to keep it that way.

CHAPTER 9

I stayed in that dumpster all night getting high. The temperature had dropped so low, I started shivering like I'd been locked in a walk in freezer. The steel that surrounded me became my tomb, I just wouldn't die. I was high, higher than I'd ever been, and still I wanted more. I was chasing that first high, a high I would never get, but somehow the devil made believe I would.

Within hours I had smoked almost 40 dime bags of crack. My heart was beating so fast and loud, I could hear it outside of my body. The cold wind whipped inside the dumpster against my body as if I was naked. I had 4 bags left, but there was no way I was gonna smoke them there, my fingers were too cold to strike the lighter. My feet were numb, and I couldn't feel them inside my shoes, it was like I didn't have any. I was beginning to sober up, and if I didn't get outta that dumpster soon I was gonna freeze to death.

It felt funny trying to stand on my feet and I couldn't feel them. Somehow I manage to climb out without hurting myself. It was about 5 o'clock in the morning, bitter cold, and the streets were quiet and deserted. I walked down the alley as the high came down and the reality of my messed up life psychologically took over. Depression set in when suddenly I realized I had nowhere to go, no family and no one who gave a damn about me. The devil was doing what he usually did, making me feel like I had no purpose for living, pushing me toward that next hit, keeping me captive, a hostage to his love potion, it was my only escape from the mad\ness that mentally tormented me. I didn't need to die to experience hell, I was already there, I was living it with my eyes wide open.

The cubby hole was not an option this day, it was much too cold to be sleeping outside. I found one of the boarded up apartment buildings in the neighborhood and broke in, at least I would be inside. Every window and entrance was boarded up, keeping the cold and violent wind from getting in. Dirty clothes, and empty crack bags were everywhere in every room of the apartment. The bathtub and toilet was filled with human waste. Bottles of urine were scattered throughout the dining room area. Rats the size of alley cats were running through the apartment in search of food. This wasn't the first time I'd been there to rest my worn out body. In the summer time it was one of my favorite spots to get high. But this was the first time I'd actually been there sober. The first time I actually noticed how filthy it was. I remember thinking to myself, "how bad my addiction had gotten." Just when I thought I was at my lowest, the devil had taken me lower.

One of the bedrooms had been swept out by someone. It had an old dirty mattress lying in the corner of the room. I was glad the room had a door, maybe that would keep the rats out. Even though it was winter time, there was a strange feeling of warmth that filled the room. That was the first time I acknowledged God was watching over me. He was keeping me in the midst of my madness.

If only I'd had the strength to listen to him, to follow him, but my will was weak. I had been defeated, deceived, cunned, and led astray down a dark and erie path of self-destruction. Lost in the grips of false joy, blind hope, and a love for a substance that didn't love me back.

I believed in God, I knew he was real, but the drugs had me trapped in a world where God didn't exist, at least that's what I told myself. I had eliminated God from the fight the very first hit, and didn't even know it. I mean, don't get me wrong, I heard that voice speaking to me, telling me right from wrong; but I just fanned it off the way a child fanned away his mother's instructions.

I laid down on the mattress and stared up at the ceiling. The apartment was quiet, except for the tiny pitty pat of rats running around in the next room. The silence settled my mind, and all of my misery came rushing back. Every bit of painful emotion caused by my addiction attacked my conscious all at once. I cried like I never cried before, reaching out with both hands, calling for my mother, wishing she could embrace me just one more time, and all would be well. I needed her now more than ever, but she was gone, and I blamed myself for her death.

I closed my eyes and tried to drift off to sleep, but the devil continued to punish me with every evil thought of my worthless life. I tried to pray, but he blocked my efforts. Every thought of God was wiped out by an evil thought of him. He was in charge, and I gave him all the power he needed to control me, there was no fight in me. The bell had rung, the gloves were off, and there was no telling what the next round would bring.

The remaining four bags of crack started to call my name while I laid helpless against the prince of darkness. I needed that high. It was my only escape from the whirlwind of emotions I was feeling. The drug was my friend, it was all I had, it was my family, my go to for comfort and companionship. It was the only thing I had to turn to,and now I needed it again.

I laid the four bags of crack on the bedroom floor, and stared at them; hesitating, trying to find the strength to resist the urge to feed my demon. The cravings were strong and demanding! My thirst for the high was unquenchable!

I stood up and backed away from the rock, but the whispers of evil got louder in my mind as though the devil was physically in the room with me. He was closer than he'd ever been before, I could feel his presence.

Suddenly, the room seemed smaller, the darkness seemed darker. I couldn't see the door anymore, nor could I see my hands as I held them up to my face. I put my hands out in front of me, feeling for the wall. I wasn't high, this was reality. I was completely sober and scared shitless!

I placed my back against the wall and stood there like a stiff board, scared to move! I wanted to get the hell outta there, but I was too afraid to open the door. This was my chance to confront the real me, I wasn't under the influence of the high and maybe, just maybe, I'd be able to think with a clear head, if I could only keep away from those last four bags long enough.

I covered my ears with both hands, trying to mute the whispers from the devil that continued to torture me. He was determined to keep me in bondage by feeding the demon that dwelled deep inside me. The demon he had awakened in my soul at the very foundation of my father's alcohol abuse. The demon he had disguised in the material love of my mother's revelation. Yes, I was there! Right there. Somewhere in the midst of free will, with not enough strength to cling to God.

And suddenly, the silence was no more as I dropped to my knees in the darkness, searching for the only friend I knew, the crack. The voices became audible, calling me to my freedom wrapped in a small piece of plastic. It was the only thing I needed to keep me from going insane. "Or was I already insane?" I was in an abandoned building, homeless in the middle of winter, infested with rats, crawling around on the floor looking for a rock that brought me nothing but a false sense of hope. But, still I trusted it to rescue me, to save me from my next thought of failure.

This wasn't a dream, this was reality, I was insane! I wasn't hgh. I was completely aware of my actions. I was mentally messed up and physically worn out! My conception of life was twisted. The truth was my enemy and every lie became my friend.

I remember thinking, "had I been insane my entire life, and somehow didn't know it?" It was so hard for me to believe my mind had left the premises without notice. I needed somebody or something to blame, but there was nothing but me. There was no reassurance, no more deniel, it was upfront and personal. The devil was trying to kill me, and he was doing it by my own hand.

I found the four bags of crack and opened one. For the first time the thought of the intensity of the high scared me, I hesitated. I struck my lighter, staring at the rock in my hand before I put it on my pipe like it was my first time. I wanted it, my body craved it, but my short lived sobriety was fighting for my life.

I tried hard to find the strength to hold on until God showed up. I felt his presence in the room, but I needed something more from him. I needed to hear his voice. I needed to see him, or touch him, or maybe he could touch me. Anything to let me know he was there.

But nothing happened! The darkness swallowed me up as I kneeled on the floor clutching the rock in my hand. I placed it on my pipe and lit it one more time. The tears ran down my face as the drug entered my system sending my soul to hell!

The effects of the high were different this time. It wasn't that peace and serenity I usually felt after. It was evil, demonic and disturbing! I felt trapped inside my own mind surrounded by demons clawing at my sanity, shredding my conscience and burning my faith. I dropped the pipe, eyes wide open gazing into the darkness unable to see. I stood on my feet, striking the still black air with both hands, swinging violently at my invisible enemy. He was there, yes, he was there. He had always been there from the very beginning. I saw him destroy my parents, and now he was after me. But just like my parents, I was helpless against his attack, he was in my head, bringing all of my misery to reality.

The voices were loud in my mind, they seemed to be speaking in many different languages and they came from every direction in the room. I was surrounded by them. They flooded the darkness and erased God's presences. My subconscious summoned God, but hell had claimed my soul.

I was there, I was in a physical hell above ground! The room held no light, the darkness revealed no exit. The drugs had exposed me to his maker and the high had led me directly to him.

I stood there, tearing off my clothes like a madman! I screamed at God, begging him to deliver me from my torment. But the demons were more powerful than they'd ever been! My body craved death as a final punishment, but my mind refused to obey. It was as if I could feel the fire but I just couldn't see it. It was attached to every part of me, and it wouldn't let go. It was real! In my mind it was all so surreal. My disobedience had nourished him, my behavior molded him, and now my mind had brought him into existence. He was there, right there in the room with me, and I had to face him in total darkness.

Satan, The Devil, Lucifer, The Beast, The Prince of Darkness, he was all of those, created by the same God I cried out to. The same God I'd been taught to put my trust in. But how could I trust him when I was being tormented by something he created.

CHAPTER 10

I don't remember how I got outta that room, or outta that building. But I do know that night did something to me mentally that I will never forget. What I experienced in that room was real, every episode of it!

Sad to say my experience wasn't enough to change my life. I should've been running as fast as I could toward the nearest church. The high had taken my mind to a horrible place, the fun was over. My best friend had turned against me and joined forces with the rest of my demons.

I remember waking up in the alley a few blocks from the building I was in. My shirt was torn half way off my body and my shoes were united. I didn't have on a coat or gloves and the bottom of my pants were ripped to the knee. At first I wanted to believe it had all been a terrible nightmare, but the evidence was there. My appearance confronted reality and the truth could not be denied, it happened!

My body was sore and exhausted. I felt completely drained physically and mentally. I had bruises all over my arms and legs as if something had beaten me. I tried to stand as the pain surged through my body from the soles of my feet to the top of my head. I felt like a runaway slave who had been caught and punished for fleeing for his freedom. Hell, I was a slave, but my master's punishment was much worse than any human.

I don't know how long I had been in that alley, but I remember being really confused. My surroundings were the same, I was in a familiar place, but for some reason things looked different. It was still 63rd street, but the scenery was altered. I didn't know what to think; "was I still high?" There was no way the effects of the drug lasted that long.

I tried to walk but my legs were aching badly from the beating I took in that dark room. My hands were swollen, my arms felt heavy and weighed down. I was too weak, I couldn't take another step. I sat down on the cold concrete, and leaned my back against the garage behind me.

I sat there for hours thinking back to where it all started. Trying to find a reason for the life I'd chosen. Looking for some sane excuse to the madness I allowed to become my destiny. Over and over in my mind I watched myself grow from a child to a man, and then addict. I saw the good times turn to bad, and the bad times get worse; but still I did nothing to stop it. My body was imprisoned by the drug, while my subconscious stored the memories that continued to torment me. My mind became a book where my demons wrote their own scriptures that I would live by. My faith in God was no more as evil resided sending me in search of my next hit!

My spirituality had been scared by the real presence of fire and brimstone, and yet my body craved another hit. My mind intoxicated with memories of a decayed life, as I patted my pockets in search of those last three bags.

Mentally I was in no condition to execute reasonable judgement. The three bags of crack called me, and I had no strength to resist them, nor did I possess the courage to challenge the evil they contained.

I sat against the garage like a helpless little boy while the demons danced and celebrated on the surface of my mind for the capture of my soul. They rewrote the purpose for my life, and sent me blindly back into the fight. It was all happening in my head while my flesh was being prepped to obey. I had toyed with the edge of sanity for too long, and now insanity had claimed its territory.

I was frightened to death of the life that awaited me. Now that my mind had surrendered to an unholy force, there was no predicting what would happen next, I had no control. I couldn't think for myself, I couldn't rationalize choices, I couldn't reason with doubt. My past revealed only what it was instructed to show me, therefore leaving no one to blame but me. The tears glided down my face, as self-pity pushed forward bringing with it unbearable grief.

This was a different avenue to the horrors of addiction. Eating outta garbage cans, sleeping in abandoned buildings, those were pitfalls I was used to. But this hostile takeover of my mentality was a first for me. Was my mind rooted in this new place? Was my flesh governed by it's leadership? Was this some form of possession? Was this the results of years of drug abuse; if so, would it take just as long to reconnect with serenity?

The sun was starting to set, and I could feel the temperature declining. The cold winter breeze gave me a sample of the brutal evening to come. I stood on my feet and started to walk, fighting back the pain with each step. I was cold and hungry, but I had to keep moving, I was sober and reality and I didn't click under those circumstances. Being high always compensated for the missed meals and cold weather. I needed a hot meal, and begging for change was not an option without a coat to keep me warm.

I kept walking until I reached Burger King. I went inside, and took a seat next to the window. I hadn't eaten in days, and the smell of the flamed broiled burgers watered my mouth, as my stomach began to cramp badly from hunger pains.

I was a mess. My shirt was torn, my pants were ripped, and I reeked of personal hygiene neglect. But then I noticed, the voices had stopped. My mind had somehow silenced itself from the mental torment. I took a deep breath, and released the stress it left behind. Suddenly, sleep washed over me as my eyelids sealed my sight while my body shut down.

I don't know how long I had been asleep, but I remember waking up feeling well rested with a tray of food sitting on the table right in front of me. But the cravings for crack woke up with me, trying to disturb the nurishment my body so badly needed. The urge was strong, and convincing. The desire for the high came without notice as it often did before that first hit. My appetite readjusted itself to a substance rather than food.

I got up from the table, the drug was calling me back out into the cold winter night. Again I had turned the cross upside down, and ignored God's blessings. But, somewhere inside of me I could hear his voice telling me, "son be still and listen."

It had been years since I was able to determine the voice of good over evil, but it was him, it was God's voice, and I knew it. I sat back down in my seat, and tried to focus on his instructions. My body felt relaxed and calm; and for the moment I wasn't scared anymore. He was there, waiting for my decision. I had to choose him, but my faith was weak. Everything I knew about God was a distant memory.

Deep in the confines of my spirit was the man he created me to be. But, the circumstances and events that plagued my life warranted a different purpose; I was an addict, and no matter how God spoke to me, the condemnation of evil wasn't ready to let me go. It had me, hook, line,and sinker, and God's voice just wasn't enough to change my mind.

I gazed at the surroundings outside with defeat in my eyes. I could feel the calmness and relaxation slipping away, while God's voice faded into the distance. I began to cry as fear found an entrance and disturbed my brief moment of peace. It was starting again, just as it always did when God was trying to get my attention. The cravings were coming, I could feel it in the pit of my stomach, while I sat there glued to the thought of getting high.

I hated not being able to control my thinking, but years of drug abuse had beaten me into submission. I was under the influence of forces beyond my understanding, and my thirst for the high filed every inch of me, I was in the grips of free will once again. It was like a turf war going on in my head; God introduced me to his salvation, while the devil stood firmly at the entrance to paradise.

I stood on my feet and prepared to meet the cold night air that awaited me. I didn't realize I had gone that entire day without a hit. Facing the realities of life with a sober mind was something I wasn't used to. I always had that false sense of security to get me through the rough times, it was an advantage the high gave me. Crack had a way of making self-destruction look like a normal day at the park.

I left Burger King that night looking for a place to lay my head. It was something I had to do everyday of my life. I remember thinking about the days when I was just a young man without a worry in the world. Both of my parents were alive, and my father's drinking hadn't turned him into a monster. Those were days I idolized my brother and sister for their accomplishments. Those were the days when all I had to do was get good grades and keep my room clean. But now, those days were just distant memories of a life stolen by the consequences of time. The challenges of life had left me vulnerable to the devices of the devil.

There weren't many options when it came to finding shelter in the neighborhood I was in. 63rd street had its share of abandoned buildings, but most of them were either boarded up, or being watched by the police. Drug addicts weren't the only ones who used the dwellings, drug dealers also frequented the properties to bag up their drugs.

Sometimes I would get lucky and find a building that still had running hot water and electricity. Those were the ones you really had to be careful in, the neighbors and the police kept a close watch on them.

I thought about going back to the building I'd been in the previous night, it was cold and not having on a coat or gloves made it feel twice as bad. That was the part I hated most about my addiction, being homeless was stressful. Walking the streets all day and night with nowhere to go drove me insane while my family slept in their warm beds and their bellies full.

The building was a block away. As much as I hated to go in there again, I didn't have much of a choice, I had to get inside, my hands and feet were getting numb, and my legs started to weaken as I fought my way through the blistering wind. By the time I reached the building, I felt like an icicle dangling from a frozen tree.

I hesitated before going into the building. The thought of the experience I had rattled my nerves. My circumstances had led me back to the horrors that awaited me. The building was calm and quiet. I stepped through the threshold of the back door with my fists balled up as though I expected to be confronted by something or someone. It was dark, I couldn't see a thing. My mind started to wonder as I felt my way through the darkness, looking for the room I was in. I ;d been sober all day, and now the cravings started again. I struck my lighter, and right in front of me was the room I'd been in the previous night. The hair stood up on my arms as I walked into the room where I nearly had a total mental breakdown.

I closed the door and sat down in the corner of the room next to the dirty mattress. The stench of urine reeked all around me, as the reality of my failures reminded me of who I'd become. I remember sitting on that floor thinking about the first time I got high. The feeling I got felt good, and it seemed harmless. But now I was in a nightmare with my eyes wide open.

Suddenly, my trip down memory lane was interrupted by the thought of those three bags. I tried hard to fight the temptation to get high, but I was hooked, I was no match for the drug, it had me.

I struck my lighter, and held the flame close to the floor as I crawled around the room on my knees looking for the crack. I couldn't believe I was sober, and there I was, crawling around on the floor in the dark looking for drugs.

It didn't take long for me to find the three bags lying next to the mattress, it was right where I left it. I picked them up and stared at them. I remember thinking, "how could something so small have so much power!" I sat with my back against the wall, as I opened one and prepared to take that trip back to insanity.

CHAPTER 11

73

I woke up face down in the middle of the floor. I didn't even remember going to sleep or getting high. My body was so worn down, I must have passed out. The three bags of crack were gone, and the pipe and lighter was lying on the floor next to me.

For the first time, I didn't remember getting high, nor did I remember the feeling, my mind was blank. It startled me for the moment, that had never happened before. Something had protected me in my helpless state. That's when I knew God was there. Even in the midst of all my misery, he was there watching over me.

I left the building that morning feeling safe. The cravings were gone, and the urge to get high wasn't there; for me that was a miracle! All those years I spent getting high seemed like a nightmare, and I'd finally woken up. But, I wasn't about to let the devil deceive me again, my life was a mess, and I knew it was all real.

I spent the rest of the day doing what I usually do, hustle to feed my addiction. I wanted to stay sober, but the pain of my past was just too much to deal with. I needed it just one more time, and I promised God if he woke me up sober I would never do drugs again.

That winter night I stood in front of 711 begging for change. I will never forget that night, It was snowing and raining at the same time. The vicious wind blew violently against my body, bringing with it a mixture of water and ice. But, the weather was no match for the desire to get high. I stepped inside 711 to count my change. I had made 20 dollars less than an hour, just enough for 2 bags. I had made a promise to God, and I planned to keep it. This would be my last night getting high. I was determined to get sober or die trying.

Mona was the third shift cashier at 711, and she had been on my heels for months about getting my life together. God was using her to get to me, and I knew it. She was like my guardian angel, she never gave up on me.

That night was the last night I would suffer from drug abuse......

It was about 2 in the morning when I made the decision to get some help. The cold snow and rain had beat against my body until I was soaking wet from my feet to the top of my head. There was no way I was gonna spend another night homeless, I was fed up!

I got on the bus that night, and rode it downtown to the Pacific Garden Mission, a shelter for the homeless. I was done, my addiction had kicked my ass for the last time! I walked into the shelter that night broken, hungry and tired.

For over 20 years I had been a hostage to the devil's love potion, a slave to a man made substance. A victim to the demons that nearly drove me insane! My addiction had brought me to my knees, I surrendered and gave the fight to God.

The staff at the shelter welcomed me with open arms. They gave me clean clothes, and something to eat, but the most beautiful part was the way they prayed for me, it was unconditional and powerful, and I received it all. God was opening doors, and I was ready to walk through them.

The following morning the shelter held church service in the auditorium. I had never seen so many homeless people come together and praise God. Many of them were drug addicts like me. Some even got up and gave their testimonies, sharing how God had freed them from the clutches of addiction. Most of their stories were similar to mine, but some of them had done things I never thought about doing to feed their habits. But, one thing we all had in common was the pain,the guilt, the misery, the self-pity, those were things we all could relate to. We had all been to war with the devil, and survived.

I sat quietly as I gazed around the room looking at the lives drugs had destroyed. Some were doctors, lawyers, successful business men, people who had worked all their lives just to have drugs take everything from them. For the first time I wasn't ashamed of who I'd become, I knew I was right where I was supposed to be. God had led me there, and I was ready to let him in.

After service that morning we all lined up in the hallway and headed to the dining room. The smell of biscuits and bacon filled the air and I was ready to fill my stomach. The tables were set, and the food was served. It was like an all you can eat restaurant, they let us eat until we had enough.

I had never seen so many drug addicts smiling, laughing and having a good time. I was in a room filled with hundreds of years of drug abuse and we were all finally sober for the moment. God was at work, and if only for that day, we were all a miracle.

CHAPTER 12

The Pacific Garden Mission was more than just a shelter, it was a blessing from God. It not only gave us clean clothes to wear, shoes to put on our feet, coats to put on our backs, food to eat, and a place to sleep. It was a spiritual setting with a Men's Bible Program on the third floor. Like I said, I was right where I needed to be.

The very next day I joined The Men's Bible Program and moved to the third floor with the rest of the students. It was a dormitory set-up with men from all walks of life with one common purpose, to serve God.

Finally, I got my chance to feel "normal," a chance to think clearly without the distraction of drugs. A chance to talk about the hurt and the pain with people who understood me. For years I buried all those ill feelings that aided in destroying my life. But, now I was in a place where I could let it all out.

I must admit, it wasn't easy talking about what I'd been through, but it felt good to be able to face those emotions without the aid of drugs. I never thought recovery for me was possible, until I joined the Men's Bible Program. Going to class everyday gave me hope, while I listened to the pastors who had faced their own struggles in life and overcame them. I was glad to know I didn't have to die in the horrors of addiction.

I went to class faithfully and sat in the front row. I wanted to make sure I didn't miss a thing. Each class was an hour long, it went by so fast, I wanted more. The pastors gave us each the opportunity to share our experiences with each other. It was something I needed to do, I needed to dump some of the garbage I was carrying around, and I was in the right place to do it.

I remember thinking to myself, "where was this place 20 years ago." I didn't wanna give the devil a chance to put doubt in my mind about the decision I made to be there, so I quickly dismissed those thoughts.

I spent 8 months in the Men's Bible Program where I worked in the barbershop cutting hair for the homeless. I gained my weight back and my sanity. I passed my eighth month test, and prepared to transition back into society. I was ready, filled with the word of God and dressed in his armour. I had finally found something that felt better than crack, the presence of God.

After leaving the bible program I checked myself into Madden Mental Hospital. The drugs had a strong psychological effect on me and I wanted to make sure I got all the help I needed. Hearing the voices of the demons in my head was real to me, and I wasn't ashamed to admit it. 20 plus years of drug abuse had definitely done something to me mentally.

Being at the mental hospital gave me a rude awakening. I didn't know how bad crack could mess with the mind until I met people there who had gone through drug abuse, and totally lost their minds. Some of them walked around like zombies, while others sat in corners talking to themselves. It was a scary experience for me, but a real one. Yes, the power of crack was devastating, but the love of God was unmatched!

I left the hospital a month later and moved into a hotel on the southwest side of Chicago. The hospital had set me up with a program called, Threshold," who helped people like me transition back into society.

I remember lying on my back in the hotel room, staring up at the ceiling, thanking God for freeing me from the grips of active addiction, thanking him for a warm bed to sleep in, thanking him for food to eat, but most of all, thanking him for my sanity. It had taken me 20 plus years to find God, and I wasn't about to let him go.

I read my bible and had my talks with God everyday. My relationship with him became strong, while I learned to use his word to fight off the advances of the devil. Getting sober was the easy part, staying sober was the ultimate test of sobriety. Each day, the devil tested me mentally. He tried repeatedly to test my faith in God, but each time I stood firm and resisted him. The more I rebelled, the stronger I became. My faith in God grew with each victory. My past no longer had a hold on me, I was free from the bondage of addiction.

I left the hotel three months later and moved in with my best friend in Hickory Hills illinois. Although I was sober, I knew I wasn't completely cured. Addiction was something I was gonna have to live with the rest of my life, it is a day by day process.

Hickory Hills was just where I needed to be. It was away from the inner city, and quiet. The peacefulness gave me a chance to get my thoughts together without any distractions. I spent a lot of time reading my Quran and Bible, and staying in prayer. Building a personal relationship with God was my primary purpose.

I had fought demons the majority of my life. I watched them destroy my parents marriage, and divide my family, turning one against the other. The reality of the devil was a bold, personal and frightening experience. I gave my life to God and got in the passenger seat.

A few months later I met Yvette Coleman, She was just what I needed. She was spiritually inclined, and a great role model. We took walks around the lake behind the building we lived in, and shared our stories with one another. I wasn't quite ready to share my struggles with addiction yet, it was personal between me and God.

She was about 5' 7" with a smooth caramel complexion that complimented those deep dimples and beautiful smile with those snow white teeth. Spiritually guided and beautiful, it was a combination that could have only been sent by God. She didn't know it, but she came into my life at the right time.

Escaping that nightmare wasn't easy, those first 30 days, I had cravings and urges you wouldn't believe. Everyday was a challenge, but I stayed focused and kept my head in that word. My talks with Yvette helped me in ways she will never know. Her theological approach was strong and committed. Being in her company gave me a warm sense of security, she knew God and she wasn't afraid to share it with me. She studied the bible with diligence, she was a soldierette in the army of the lord, and I wanted what she had.

I remember telling her, "God told me you're the one," she looked at me and said, "well, he hasn't told me anything." We laughed until it brought tears to our eyes. I hadn't laughed like that in years, it was a feeling I welcomed with open arms.

As the days passed, I got closer and closer to God. Yvette and I started dating, I guess she finally got the o.k. from up above. It was nice to have someone in my life who laid a positive path for me to follow. We both had our struggles, but we were determined to build something together. It wasn't the first time I'd been sober, but this time I had to succeed, relapsing was not an option. I was ready to do whatever it took to leave that life in my past.

Six months later Yvette and I got married, that was the best decision I could've made. By this time, I had a year clean, and the blessings of God came pouring in. I didn't have a lot of money, but I had something money couldn't buy, I had peace, serenity, a praying wife, and a relationship with the one who created me.

I joined New Memorial Baptist Church on the southside of Chicago, and started my own ministry, cutting hair every Saturday, free for anyone that wanted it. It was my way of giving back something positive, a chance to share the word of GOD with the young men who sat in my chair every weekend. The feeling I got from serving God was unexplainable. It's something every human being should experience.

God had taken away the temptation, the cravings, the urges, it was all gone. My mind was free from mental torment. My body was loosened from physical neglect. My thoughts were pure and protected by the grace of God. My misery was deleted, and replaced with joy. FINALLY, MY RACE TO HELL WAS OVER!

EPILOGUE

83

Mental madness, misery, guilt, physical neglect; it all came like a whirlwind as I crawled around in the darkness, searching for my sanity. I had barricaded myself in the cold bedroom of the condemned building. The demons danced on the surface of mind, bringing with them the illusion of peace in a small rock that my body craved for. It was hell dressed like heaven at the end of my glass pipe. It promised to rescue me from all that tormented me, while reality slipped away at the strike of my lighter. It seemed that not even God could save me from the bottom in which I was headed.

It was my turn to wrestle with the prince of darkness, and his appointed legions of entities. My faith had been bottled up and sealed shut, leaving my soul stained in the pits of HELL!

ABOUT THE AUTHOR

Derrick Turner was born and raised on the southside of Chicago. He is the youngest of four children. He attended Hyde Park Career Academy, and graduated in 1985, and then he continued his studies in Fine Arts and Creative Writing at Columbia College of Chicago.

After college, Derrick struggled with drug addiction for over 20 years; until 2009 when God freed him from self-destruction and set him on a path of recovery. He joined the Men's Bible Program at The Pacific Garden Mission in Chicago.

In 2017, Derrick wrote and published his first book, titled, Finding Peace, "escape from a self-made hell." He went on to write and publish 6 more books, as his passion to become an author grew with each book.

Derrick has been clean and sober for 12 years. He continues to write and share his real life stories with his readers. He hopes to touch the lives of those who fight the disease of addiction everyday.

www.ingramcontent.com/pod-product-compliance
Lightning Source LLC
Chambersburg PA
CBHW031033190726
48286CB00003BA/1159